THE STARS AND STRIPES

The Story of Our Flag

BY IRVING WERSTEIN

GOLDEN PRESS 🦅 NEW YORK

PICTURE CREDITS

p. 8 Painting by Alton S. Tobey for *The Golden Book History of the United States;* p. 12 Yale University Art Gallery; p. 14 Dixon *Ticonderoga* Pencil Collection; p. 17 John Trumbull, *Declaration of Independence,* Yale University Art Gallery; p. 18 (top) *Universal History of the World,* Golden Press; (bottom) John Trumbull, *Capture of the Hessians at Trenton,* Yale University Art Gallery: p. 21 (top) I. N. Phelps Stokes Collection, The New York Public Library, Astor, Lenox and Tilden Foundations; (bottom) Emmet Collection, The New York Public Library, Astor, Lenox and Tilden Foundations; p. 22 (top) U.P.I.; (bottom) Valley Forge Historical Society; p. 27 (top) Rome, N.Y. Historical Society; (bottom) The Bennington Museum, Bennington, Vermont; p. 28 John Trumbull, *The Surrender of General Burgoyne,* Yale University Art Gallery; p. 31 Frederick Kemmelmeyer, *The Battle of Cowpens,* Yale University Art Gallery, Mabel Brady Garven Collection; p. 32 The Pierpont Morgan Library; p. 36 Painting by Alton S. Tobey for *The Golden Book History of the United States;* p. 38 State Capitol, Richmond, Virginia; p. 44 New York Historical Society; pp. 46, 52-53, Paintings by Alton S. Tobey for *The Golden Book History of the United States;* p. 56 American Heritage (courtesy Reverend DeWolf Perry; p. 58 Frederick Hill Meserve Collection; p. 61 Courtesy of the Galena Historical Society, Galena, Illinois; p. 64 Copyright 1945, The Associated Press; Pictures on pp. 12, 14, 17, 18 (bottom), 21, 22 (bottom), 27, 28, 31, 32, appeared in *The Golden Book of the American Revolution* adapted for young readers from *The American Heritage Book of the Revolution;* Pictures on p. 44 appeared in *The Golden Book of America* adapted for young readers from *American Heritage.*

Cover art by Adelson and Eichinger Inc.
Flag illustrations by William Sayles

CONTENTS

America's First Flags   9

The Grand Union   15

The Stars And Stripes   20

The Stars And Stripes In Land Combat   26

The Stars And Stripes At Sea   33

Salutes And Confusion   39

Fifteen Stars And Stripes   42

The Star-Spangled Banner   47

A New Flag Law   50

Old Glory   54

The Flag And The Civil War   59

The Flag In War And Peace   62

The Use Of The Flag   66

The Vikings brought the first flags to the New World.

The sun never sets on the American flag. It flies over American embassies and consulates, over military posts, camps, garrisons, and stations in every corner of the world; it flies from naval and merchant ships on the seven seas. Even at the ends of the earth, in the regions of the North Pole and the South Pole, the flag is unfurled.

The flag played a part in American history—and it has a history of its own. That history began with the coming of Europeans to America, for the original inhabitants, the American Indians, had no flags. It was the discoverers, the explorers, the adventurers, and the settlers from Europe who brought the first flags to the New World.

Earliest to arrive were the Vikings, in about 1000 A.D. The flag they carried showed a black raven, with wings outstretched, on a white field. Not for five centuries did another flag appear in the New World. Then, in 1492, Christopher Columbus raised the red and white flag of Spain on an island in the Bahamas which he named San Salvador. Five years later, the explorer John Cabot sighted some islands off the coast of North America, probably near Cape Breton or Newfoundland. His ship carried the English flag, which bore the red cross of St. George, and he claimed the land for King Henry VII. The French flag, with its fleur-de-lis, was brought to North America in 1534, when Jacques Cartier sailed up the Gulf of St. Lawrence and claimed a vast area for King Francis I.

By the seventeenth century, both France and England had large holdings in North America. The English flag waved over settlements along the Atlantic seaboard, including Jamestown, which was settled in 1607, and Plymouth, which was settled in 1620. The French, who

America's First Flags

VIKING FLAG

SPANISH FLAG

9

BRITISH FLAG

FRENCH FLAG

DUTCH FLAG

RED ENSIGN

called their territory New France, founded colonies at Quebec in 1608 and at Montreal in 1642. From these colonies trappers and traders carried the French flag south and west, and France soon claimed the lands from the St. Lawrence to New Orleans.

There were other flags, too, in North America. In 1623 the Dutch raised their orange, white, and blue banner over the province of New Netherland, along the banks of the Hudson River. Three years later they founded New Amsterdam, at the southern tip of Manhattan Island. The Swedish flag, a gold cross on a blue field, waved for a brief time over the colony of New Sweden on the Delaware River. In 1655, seventeen years after its founding, the colony was overrun by the Dutch. The Swedish flag was replaced by the Dutch flag, whose colors had been changed to red, white, and blue.

Any hope the Dutch may have had for an American empire was shattered in 1664, when a British fleet captured New Amsterdam. The British promptly renamed the settlement New York. Over it they raised the British flag known as the Red Ensign. This had a red field with a canton—or upper inner corner—consisting of the red cross of St. George, patron saint of England, combined with the white cross of St. Andrew, patron saint of Scotland, the two crosses representing the union of the two countries.

At the end of the seventeenth century, France and Britain remained the chief rivals for the control of North America. They fought three indecisive wars between 1689 and 1748, but in the French and Indian War, which lasted from 1754 to 1763, the French were defeated. The Red Ensign flew unchallenged over thirteen British colonies. Before long, however, each of them also had its own flag. The colonists were British subjects, and they had no intention of giving up the Red Ensign, but they needed flags to identify the ships of the individual colonies. Ships from Massachusetts, for example, flew a flag bearing a green pine tree on a white field. Ships from New York carried a white flag with a black beaver, which represented the colony's profitable fur trade.

As disputes broke out between the colonies and the mother country—disputes that would in time lead to the Revolutionary War and the establishment of a new nation—the angry colonists sewed or pasted slogans on the Red Ensign. In 1774, the people of Taunton, Massachusetts, hoisted an Ensign embroidered with these words: "Liberty and Union." A Pennsylvania militia company carried an Ensign on which was sewn a rattlesnake over the warning: "Don't Tread On Me." More and more such flags appeared. Most of them bore the emblem of the rattlesnake or the pine tree, and a number of them the slogan, "Liberty or Death!"

In April of 1775 the first shots fired in the war rang out at Lexington and Concord. By June 17, the embattled Americans were entrenched on Breed's Hill and Bunker Hill, just outside Boston. Two flags flew over the earthworks. One, a blue banner with a pine tree and the cross of St. George, became known as the Bunker Hill Flag. The other became known as the Continental Flag. It was red, with a white canton, or upper inner quarter. On the canton was a pine tree.

It was the Pine Tree flag, in varying designs, that flew over the cannon aimed at the British in Boston. And it was the Pine Tree that served as the first American naval flag. In the fall of 1775, six small ships were fitted out as men-of-war. Each flew a white flag with a green pine tree and the motto: "An Appeal To Heaven."

This flag was made official on April 29, 1776, when the General Court of Massachusetts ordered the fleet to fly "a white Flagg with Green Pine Tree and the motto 'An Appeal to Heaven.'" Although the Court clearly described the flag, ship captains changed it as they

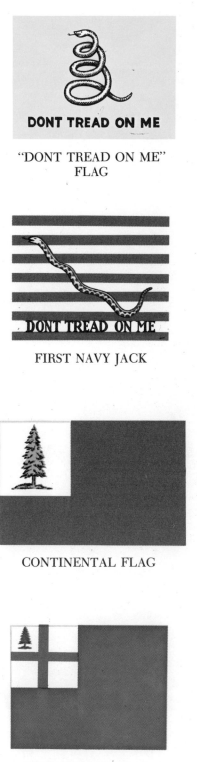

"DONT TREAD ON ME"
FLAG

FIRST NAVY JACK

CONTINENTAL FLAG

BUNKER HILL FLAG

John Trumbull's painting of the Battle of Breed's Hill, June, 1775, shows a flag with a pine tree on it.

pleased. Some did not even use the pine tree and the motto. Instead, they used the rattlesnake and "Don't Tread On Me." A few captains changed the word "heaven" in the motto to "God." While the Pine Tree flag was flown mainly at sea, several New England infantry regiments, particularly those from Massachusetts, fought under it throughout the war.

The Pine Tree Flag might have become the emblem of the thirteen colonies, except for one thing. It was too closely linked with New England to be accepted by all the colonies. During the early days of the Revolution, a number of attempts were made to design a satisfactory flag. One flag bore thirteen mailed hands grasping a chain, another a mailed fist clutching thirteen arrows. Still another showed a rattlesnake with thirteen rattles in its tail.

The first flag to use thirteen stripes to represent the colonies was the Markoe flag of the Philadelphia Light Horse Troop. It was named after its designer, Captain Abram Markoe. In the center of the yellow field was an elaborate coat of arms, and in the upper inner corner were thirteen alternate blue and silver stripes.

Stars were also used to represent the colonies. Perhaps the first to do so was the flag of the United Train of Artillery, a militia unit from Providence, Rhode Island. It, too, had a yellow field. In the center were a snake, a fouled anchor, two cannon, and a scroll with two mottoes, "Do Not Tread On Me" and "In God We Hope"—all enclosed in a circle of thirteen five-pointed stars. In February of 1776, the First Rhode Island Infantry Regiment paraded behind a white flag with thirteen stars on a blue canton. They were arranged in rows of three, two, three, two, and three.

But none of these flags seemed the proper symbol for thirteen British colonies that had united to fight for their rights. And so the search went on, until the introduction of the flag known as the Grand Union.

WASHINGTON'S
CRUISERS FLAG

MARKOE FLAG

UNITED TRAIN OF
ARTILLERY FLAG

RHODE ISLAND FLAG

*Guns brought from Fort Ticonderoga to Boston enabled
Washington to take that city in March, 1776. The Grand Union Flag
was raised there after the British troops marched out.*

14

On January 1, 1776, by order of the Continental Congress, the Continental Army, under the command of General George Washington, officially became the chief fighting force of the colonists struggling against Britain. To mark the day, a ceremony was held at Cambridge, Massachusetts. An important part of the ceremony was the raising of a flag on a 76-foot-high pole atop Prospect Hill. Washington later wrote, "We had hoisted the Union Flag in compliment to the United Colonies."

The Union Flag, as Washington called it, was also known by many other names—the Continental Flag, the Congress Flag, the Colors of the United Colonies, the Great Union, and the Grand Union. But most of the colonists called it the Grand Union.

The design of the Grand Union Flag was not original. It was exactly the same as Britain's Red Ensign, except for six white stripes running horizontally across the red field. In fact, some of the people who watched the flag-raising on Prospect Hill believed the colonists had indeed run up the Red Ensign. Among them was an observer who made a report to General William Howe, the commander of the British troops in Boston. Howe told an aide that by displaying the British flag the colonists were showing that they intended to give up.

Howe soon discovered his mistake. In March, with the Grand Union flying from his flagship, Commodore Esek Hopkins led the American fleet in a raid against New Providence, a British possession in the Bahamas. He captured 100 cannon for the poorly armed Continental Army. And that same month the Grand Union was raised in Boston, after the British troops had marched out. The next month it was raised in New York, when Washington occupied Manhattan Island and Brooklyn Heights.

Although the Continental Congress never officially adopted the Grand Union, it was regarded as the national flag by all the colonies and the fighting forces. It

The Grand Union

GRAND UNION FLAG

15

waved over forts and barracks from Massachusetts to Georgia, and flew from the masts of men-at-war, privateers, and merchant ships. It was used so widely because its design was acceptable to men from every part of the country. It stood for no particular colony.

There was another reason, too, for its popularity. At the beginning of the Revolutionary War, few colonists wanted to break away from Britain and establish a new nation. They considered themselves British, and they were demanding their rights as Britons. They hoped to win these rights and remain British subjects. They were as proud of being Britons as they were of being Americans. The Grand Union Flag expressed their mixed feelings. The cross of St. George and the cross of St. Andrew in the canton represented their link to Britain. The thirteen stripes represented the colonies in the New World.

But, as the fighting went on, the colonists became convinced that they would have to cut themselves off from Britain and form a nation of their own. And in June of 1776 the Grand Union was raised over the hall in Philadelphia where the Continental Congress met to debate independence. On July 2, 1776, the Congress voted in favor of a resolution of independence, and the Grand Union automatically became the flag of the United States of America. Two days later the Congress adopted the Declaration of Independence. But with its reminders of the past, the Grand Union was no longer a suitable flag. The new nation needed a new flag. Only the Congress, however, had the power to approve a new flag and it was too busy. For almost a year, the Grand Union continued to serve as the American flag.

On July 9, 1776, Washington ordered his troops in New York to assemble at the Battery, on the southern tip of Manhattan Island. The Declaration of Independence was read to the soldiers, who cheered and fired their muskets into the air. To the sound of fife and

Thomas Jefferson and the drafting committee submit the Declaration of Independence to the Continental Congress. After the Declaration was adopted, the Grand Union became the flag of the United States of America.

16

17

18

drums, the Grand Union was raised. British warships were anchored at the mouth of New York Bay, and an officer watched the Americans through a telescope. He wrote in his journal: "They have set up their standard in the fort upon the southern point of the town . . . Their colours are thirteen stripes of red and white alternately, with the union canton in the corner . . . It is quite the same flag as ours but for the stripes."

In the early days of the new nation, the Grand Union played a part in a variety of incidents. During October of 1776, Benedict Arnold hastily gathered a fleet of ships to meet a British threat on Lake Champlain. The Grand Union flew boldly from his flagship, the *Royal Savage,* but the flimsy American vessels were quickly sunk by the British naval squadron. The *Royal Savage* went to the bottom, and with it went the Grand Union.

A month later, the Grand Union received the first salute to an American flag from a foreign nation. Fort Orange on St. Eustatius in the Dutch West Indies thundered an eleven-gun welcome to the *Andrew Doria,* a ship in Commodore Hopkins' fleet. The Dutch were returning the courtesy of a similar salute from the American guns, but the British consul at St. Eustatius protested angrily. He said the Dutch had saluted a ship "flying the flag of His Majesty's rebellious subjects."

In December, when British forces threatened Philadelphia, the Continental Congress fled to Baltimore, first taking down the Grand Union from the staff on Independence Hall. After Washington's victories at Trenton and Princeton, the Congress returned to Philadelphia, and once more the Grand Union waved over Independence Hall. And when the Continental Army dug in at Morristown, New Jersey, in the winter of 1776–77, the flag that was raised at its headquarters was again the Grand Union.

But the Americans wanted a flag of their own, and it would not be long before the Congress took action.

John Trumbull's painting
of Washington's victory at
Trenton. This victory meant
that the Grand Union would
again wave over Independence
Hall in Philadelphia.

19

The Stars and Stripes

The spring of 1777 was a grim season for the Americans. General Sir William Howe's army took New York City, less than a hundred miles from Philadelphia, the new nation's capital. Between General Howe and the capital stood the outnumbered and ragged Continental Army. Washington's men lacked supplies and equipment, and even proper clothing. But, as the Americans and the British marched and countermarched across New Jersey, Washington managed to keep the enemy forces in check and prevented an attack on Philadelphia.

Meanwhile, the Congress was meeting daily in Independence Hall, carrying on the business of government. Bills were introduced, and laws passed. On June 14, 1777, it met as usual. The matters before it that day were not of the greatest importance; they required little discussion and could be handled by resolutions. Among them was one concerning a new national flag.

The flag resolution read:

> RESOLVED, That the flag of the thirteen United States be thirteen stripes, alternate red and white; that the union or canton be thirteen stars, white in a blue field, representing a new constellation . . .

The resolution was passed unanimously, and at last, almost a year after its birth, the nation had an official flag, a flag of its own—the Stars and Stripes. And just as the United States was different from other nations, so the flag was different from other flags.

The men who wrote the resolution creating the new flag failed to credit anyone with its design. Who he was remained a mystery, and the result was that many stories and legends sprang up about the origin of the flag.

American troops carrying the Grand Union Flag escaped when the British captured Fort Washington (above) and Fort Lee on the Hudson.

Betsy Ross, according to legend, made the first Stars and Stripes. However, there is no evidence that she actually did so.

A night attack near Philadelphia by the British on American troops during the Revolution. In 1777, Philadelphia had fallen to the British. York, Pennsylvania, was the temporary capital.

According to the best known of the legends, George Washington and several other prominent Americans formed a committee to design a national flag. In late May or early June of 1776 the group met in Philadelphia. Washington presented a colored sketch for the new flag, and the committee decided to have a sample flag made at once. To do the job, they selected Mrs. Elizabeth Ross—or Betsy Ross, as she was called—an expert seamstress. Following Washington's sketch, she stitched together a flag of thirteen stripes and thirteen stars. The stars were set in a circle on a blue canton. Washington then showed the flag to the Continental Congress, which enthusiastically approved Betsy Ross's handiwork and passed the Flag Resolution.

FIRST STARS
AND STRIPES

It is a delightful story—but it is fiction, not fact. Washington was indeed in Philadelphia during late May and early June of 1776, but he had come to discuss with the Congress the desperate situation of the Continental Army. The problems he faced made the design of a new flag relatively unimportant. Furthermore, the Congress kept a detailed record of all its activities, and there is no mention in it of a flag committee. The Betsy Ross legend can be traced to a magazine article written by her grandson in the 1850's. As for Betsy Ross, she did make flags for ships, and it is likely that she made some in the Stars and Stripes design. But there is no evidence whatever that she made the first flag.

Many years later, in 1926, another legend was set off by the discovery of a Revolutionary War flag in an old house on Long Island, New York. The house had once belonged to John Hulbert, who commanded a Long Island militia company at the start of the Revolution. The flag was supposed to be the original Stars and Stripes, presented in 1775 by Long Island patriots to Hulbert's company before it left for war. Historians proved that this was impossible. No Stars and Stripes existed before 1777. The Hulbert flag was of the Revolutionary War

HULBERT FLAG

period, but of a later date than 1777. Another belief exploded by historians is that the Stars and Stripes was based on the Washington family coat-of-arms, which bears two red stripes and three stars. Again they could find no evidence of any connection between the two designs.

Over the years, many attempts have been made to solve the mystery of the flag's designer. Candidates for this honor range from George Washington to little-known figures of the Revolutionary period. The one most frequently mentioned is Francis Hopkinson of New Jersey.

Hopkinson was a signer of the Declaration of Independence, and he enjoyed a local reputation as a writer, artist, and student of heraldry. His first claim for recognition as the designer of the Stars and Stripes was made in 1780. That year, he presented the Congress with a bill "for services rendered." It listed a number of items, including designs for "the Flag of the United States; Seven Devices for the Continental Currency; A seal for the Board of the Treasury; and A Great Seal for The United States of America." Hopkinson humorously asked as payment "a quarter cask . . . of public wine . . . which is a proper and reasonable reward for these labours of fancy . . . and a suitable encouragement to others of the like nature."

But Congress refused to recognize Hopkinson as the designer of the flag. He received neither a cask of wine nor payment of any kind. Congress simply rejected his entire bill.

Hopkinson then sent in a second bill. This time he asked for more than a cask of wine. He demanded $7,200 for designing what he termed "the Great Naval Flag of the United States." Since the so-called Great Naval Flag has always been the same as the national flag, Hopkinson was again asking for recognition as the designer of the Stars and Stripes. But again he received no recognition and no payment. After some delay, the United States Treasury Department stated that Hopkinson could not declare "exclusive authorship" of the flag, since he "was not the only person consulted" on its design.

From the evidence, it seems that Francis Hopkinson had something to do with the first Stars and Stripes, but not enough to be named and honored as its designer. Exactly who was the "Father of the American Flag" remains a mystery to this day.

If the facts of the flag's origin are clouded by legend, so are the facts of its first public raising. One legend makes the claim that a flag was sewn in time to be raised over Washington's headquarters at reveille on June 15, 1777. Another legend claims that the Stars and Stripes was first raised at an army outpost near Hubbardton, Vermont, on the same day; still another that the place was Fort Ann, New York.

Historians say that it was unlikely that the Stars and Stripes was first raised at such an early date. Although Congress passed the Flag Resolution on June 14, 1777, the resolution was not made public until September 3, 1777.

It is true, however, that news of it leaked out before the public announcement. A Philadelphian named Ezra Stiles wrote in his diary on July 9 that "I hear the Congress have substituted a Constellation of 13 stars for the Crosses of St. George and St. Andrew in the Continental Colors." Dr. James Thacher, an army surgeon stationed near Albany, New York, had more detailed information. On August 3 he made this entry in his journal: "It appears . . . that Congress Resolved on June 14th last, that the flag of the United States be thirteen stripes, alternate red and white, and that the Union be thirteen stars, white on a blue field." Perhaps it was reports like these that gave rise to the legends about the raising of the flag at an early date.

The Stars and Stripes in Land Combat

Many legends about the flag deal with its first appearance in combat on land. The most famous of these stories was not told until 1926, the 150th anniversary of the Declaration of Independence. On that date an official of the War Department stated that the Stars and Stripes had received its "baptism of fire" at the battle of Fort Stanwix, in upper New York State, on August 3, 1777. He went on to say that the besieged American troops had learned of the description of the Stars and Stripes in the Flag Resolution. They then quickly fashioned such a flag, using material from a blue cloak with a red lining, and a white shirt donated by the fort's commander, Colonel Peter Gansevoort.

Newspapers throughout the nation carried the story, and it aroused a storm of protest from historians. They agreed that the troops at the fort had fought under an improvised flag, but that it could not have been the Stars and Stripes. "Their crude flag bore stripes but no stars," one prominent historian wrote. "It was in fact the Grand Union, or a facsimile of it."

The historians also pointed out another error in the story—the name of the fort. Fort Stanwix, built in 1758, had fallen into disrepair long before the Revolution. A new fort, named for General Philip Schuyler, was built on the same site in 1776. The correct name of the fort was therefore Fort Schuyler, and not Fort Stanwix. The War Department quickly withdrew the story, but it was too late. Another legend of the flag had been created.

Most historians believe that the Battle of Bennington, which took place in Vermont on August 16, 1777, was the first land fighting to involve the Stars and Stripes. Word of the Flag Resolution had somehow reached General John Stark, the American commander, and he ordered a flag made according to the description given in the resolution. As his men marched into battle under that flag, Stark drew his sword and pointed toward the enemy troops, who were atop a hill near the town.

Another flag legend. This painting by Edward Buyck shows the raising of the new Stars and Stripes over Fort Stanwix in August, 1777. Historians say it never happened. The Battle of Bennington was probably the first on land to involve the Stars and Stripes.

A painting of the British surrender after the Battle of Saratoga shows the Stars and Stripes. However, this painting is probably not historically accurate.

29

BENNINGTON FLAG

"Tonight," he said, "the American flag floats over yonder hill or Molly Stark sleeps a widow."

By nightfall, the Stars and Stripes was floating over the hill, Molly Stark was no widow, and the British forces had been defeated.

The Bennington flag, which is preserved at the Bennington Historical Museum, is of an unusual design. Although it has thirteen stripes, the top stripe is white instead of red. The thirteen stars have six points. They are arranged on the canton to form a Gothic arch over the figure "76," which commemorates the year American independence was proclaimed.

Another story of the early use of the flag in land combat is connected with the Battle of Saratoga, which was fought in New York State in October of 1777. After the British forces, under General John Burgoyne, had surrendered, some patriotic women of the neighborhood cut up red, white, and blue flannel petticoats and made a flag. They gave the flag to General Horatio Gates, the commander of the American troops, who ordered it carried in the victory parade. It is true that General Burgoyne surrendered at Saratoga, and that the Americans won an important victory—but historians have established that the rest of the story is fiction.

There is no doubt, however, about the truth of the story of the flag that played a part in the American victory at Cowpens. On January 17, 1781, Colonel Eager Howard's Third Maryland Regiment fought against the British at Cowpens, South Carolina. Color Sergeant William Batchelor, who carried a flag of Stars and Stripes design during the battle, was wounded. He was sent to his home in Baltimore, and brought the flag with him. It remained in his family until 1907, when his descendants presented it to the state of Maryland, and the Cowpens flag is now at the State House in Annapolis.

Although a number of military units fought under the Stars and Stripes during the Revolution, they did so

COWPENS FLAG

without Congressional approval. George Washington repeatedly asked that the troops be allowed to carry the national colors, but for some reason Congress refused to grant permission until March of 1783, more than a year after the last land battle of the Revolutionary War. Even then, use of the Stars and Stripes was limited to display at forts, camps, and other military installations. It was only after 1834, when Congress at last gave its approval, that Army units could legally carry the flag in parades or in combat.

At no time during the Revolution was the Stars and Stripes the official flag of the army. It was carried at such places as Bennington and Cowpens because of men like General Stark and Colonel Howard, who understood the need of American fighting men for a battle flag of their own.

The Stars and Stripes was carried in the Battle of Cowpens.

32

Shortly after the Flag Resolution, Congress approved the use of the Stars and Stripes as the official Naval Ensign. It voted unanimously to give the Navy permission to "fly the flag of the thirteen United States." Just why it did this, when it refused to give such permission to the Army, remains unclear. Perhaps it was because there was a strong Congressional committee concerned with naval affairs; perhaps it was because of the need for ships at sea to identify themselves unmistakably.

Many of the early events involving the Stars and Stripes at sea were connected with Captain John Paul Jones, one of the greatest figures in naval history. He received his first command—the man-of-war *Ranger*—on June 14, 1777, the same day that Congress passed the Flag Resolution. He considered this significant, and felt that his life was linked in some strange way with the Stars and Stripes. He once wrote:

"The Flag and I are Twins; born the same day and the same hour . . . We cannot be parted in life or in death . . . So long as we can float, we shall float together. If we must sink, we shall go down as one!"

As might be expected, Jones was the central figure in many legends of the American flag. One legend tells about an incident that was supposed to have taken place at Portsmouth, New Hampshire. The story goes that on July 4, 1777, Jones was overseeing the final steps

The Stars and Stripes at Sea

in the construction of the *Ranger*. Five young ladies of Portsmouth presented him with a flag made from "their best silk dresses." He promptly assembled the ship's crew and raised "the beautifully sewn silken banner," amid frenzied applause and cheers from the onlookers.

The incident never happened, at Portsmouth or anywhere else. Jones was not even in Portsmouth on July fourth. He arrived there on the eleventh, and took command of the *Ranger* the next day. It is a fact, however, that when the *Ranger* sailed off for active duty on November 1, 1777, a large Stars and Stripes flew from her mainmast—the first appearance of the Stars and Stripes on the Atlantic Ocean.

A number of other "firsts" soon followed. While on the way to France, Jones captured a British war sloop, the first prize taken by a ship flying the Stars and Stripes. When the *Ranger* reached France, the French welcomed her with a nine-gun salute, the first such honor given the Stars and Stripes by a foreign power. In April of 1778, the 18-gun *Ranger* fought against the 20-gun British war sloop *Drake*. Within half an hour, Jones forced the *Drake* to strike her colors. This was the first victory in a shooting battle by a vessel flying the Stars and Stripes.

More than a year later, on September 23, 1779, came what was perhaps Jones's most famous battle. It took place off Flamborough Head, Yorkshire, England, between Jones's flagship, the 40-gun *Bonhomme Richard*, and the 50-gun British warship *Serapis*. The *Bonhomme Richard*, which was an old vessel, was soon battered by the British guns and was close to sinking. The captain of the *Serapis* signalled: "Strike your colors." Jones replied, "I have not yet begun to fight."

Instead of giving up, Jones brought the *Bonhomme Richard* alongside the enemy vessel. Wielding cutlasses, Jones and his men boarded the *Serapis*. After a brief but wild fight, the British surrendered. From the deck of the

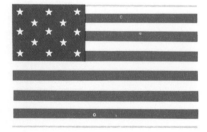

ALLIANCE FLAG

captured ship, Jones and his men watched the *Bonhomme Richard* sink beneath the waves.

Describing his ship's last moment, Jones later wrote: "The very last vestige mortal eyes ever saw of the *Bonhomme Richard* was the defiant waving of her unconquered and unstricken Flag as she went down."

From this battle sprang still another legend. Some time later, Congress was presented with a flag said to be one of those flown from the *Bonhomme Richard*. James Stafford, the donor, had been one of the crew, and he claimed to have saved the banner from a "watery grave." He also claimed that the flag of which Jones had written was only one of several which had been flown from the ship. No one, including Jones, could recall exactly how many flags the *Bonhomme Richard* had carried.

Stafford said that the flag he had rescued was the one that the Americans had raised over the captured *Serapis*. Although there was no proof of the truth of his story, the flag was placed on display at the Smithsonian Institution a number of years later. It had only twelve stars in the canton, arranged in three rows of four each. An imaginative journalist added something new to the legend. He stated that the thirteenth had been sewn on the canton apart from the rest, and that it had been removed from the flag during the Civil War and given to President Abraham Lincoln as a birthday present.

Although the Stars and Stripes was the official flag, the flags flown on the *Ranger*, the *Bonhomme Richard*, and other ships of the Navy differed widely in design. For example, an eyewitness described a flag on the *Alliance*, a ship commanded by John Paul Jones during the last months of the war, as having thirteen stars and red, white, and blue stripes. There was a great deal of confusion about the proper design of the flag, and among those who were confused were John Adams and Benjamin Franklin. In a letter written at Paris on

The battle between John Paul Jones's flagship the Bonhomme Richard
and the British ship Serapis. Jones later wrote: "The very last vestige mortal eyes
ever saw of the Bonhomme Richard was the defiant waving of her
unconquered and unstricken Flag as she went down."

October 9, 1778, and signed by both of them, they said that "the Flag of the United States of America . . . consists of thirteen stripes alternately red, white, and blue; a small square in the upper angle next the flag staff is a blue field with thirteen stars."

The confusion went on for many years. As late as 1847, the Dutch government asked the American government for "the exact pattern of the U.S. national colors so that we may pay it proper respect." It was probably the first time in history that one nation had requested such information from another.

The British surrendered to George Washington at Yorktown.

On October 19, 1781, the main British forces, under General Cornwallis, surrendered to George Washington at Yorktown, Virginia. Except for a few flare-ups of fighting, the Revolutionary War was over. By the end of 1782, the British had evacuated all the Atlantic ports they had occupied. The last of the British soldiers left New York in April of 1783, and in September of that same year a peace treaty was signed at Paris. The colonists had won their struggle for independence. The United States of America was at last a full-fledged nation, and the Stars and Stripes could take its place with the flags of other sovereign countries.

There were still many difficulties to be overcome. There was still uncertainty about the future of the United States. One sign of the uncertainty was the number of times the capital city was changed. From 1783 to 1785, the Stars and Stripes was raised over capitol buildings in Philadelphia, Princeton, Trenton, Annapolis, and New York. Yet in spite of unrest, in spite of political differences and financial troubles, the nation survived. In 1787 a Constitutional Convention met at Philadelphia and worked out a bold new plan for government. The Constitution was ratified by most of the states by 1788, and in April of the following year Washington was sworn in as the first President. The United States was a constitutionally established nation with an established government.

As the flag of an established nation, the Stars and Stripes was recognized and saluted by nations throughout the world, including the former mother country. The first peacetime voyage of an American ship to England was completed on February 3, 1783. Captain William Moers of Nantucket sailed his schooner, the *Bedford*, up the Thames estuary to London. One London newspaper said, "This is the first ship which has displayed the thirteen rebellious stripes . . . and stars of America in any British port."

Salutes and Confusion

It was not long before the East as well as the West became familiar with the American flag. The schooner *Empress of China,* sailing from New York under Captain John Greene, entered the port of Canton, China, on August 30, 1784. Captain Greene brought back a cargo of teas and silks that enriched the ship's owners. Soon other merchants were outfitting ships and carrying on a brisk trade with China.

On September 30, 1787, a Rhode Island sea captain, Robert Gray, set out from Boston on a voyage around the world. He navigated his ship, the *Lady Washington,* around Cape Horn and put in at Nootka Sound, Vancouver, Canada. There he transferred his flag to another vessel, the *Columbia.* Gray then sailed the *Columbia* around the globe, returning to Boston in August of 1790. It was the first time the Stars and Stripes had been carried around the world.

The citizens of the United States were proud of this achievement, but nothing pleased them more than an incident that took place on May 2, 1791. On that day, a British warship, the *Alligator,* put in at Boston. The captain of the vessel, Isaac Coffin, ordered a 13-gun salute to the Stars and Stripes flying from Fort Independence, which was later known as Castle William. A ship representing Britain, which had been the enemy, was honoring the United States flag, and the fort's guns boomed out a salute in return.

Although the Stars and Stripes was gaining a place for itself, there was still no agreement about its design. Many questions were still unsettled. What should be the exact size and shape of the flag? Should the stripes be horizontal or vertical? Should the stars have five, six, seven, or eight points? And how should the stars be arranged in the canton?

Today, many people mistakenly believe that the early versions of the Stars and Stripes bore stars arranged in a circle. This belief can be traced to paintings done by artists who disregarded historical accuracy. The first of such paintings was Charles Weisberger's *The Birth of Our Nation's Flag.* It depicted Betsy Ross busily sewing a banner supposed to be the original Stars and Stripes. Weisberger arranged the stars in a circle simply because he thought they looked better that way.

TRUMBULL FLAG

Two other famous paintings also show the stars in a circle. They are *The Spirit of '76* by A. M. Willard and *Washington Crossing the Delaware* by Emanuel Leutze. If the painters had done sufficient research, they would have known that the Stars and Stripes did not even exist in 1776. Leutze might also have realized that Washington would never have stood up in a crowded rowboat while making a dangerous crossing of a river filled with floating ice. Both these pictures were painted long after the Revolution. John Trumbull, a prominent painter of the Revolutionary period, showed an entirely different arrangement of the stars in his paintings of scenes of the war. On the cantons of the flags he depicted, twelve stars are arranged in a hollow square, with a thirteenth star in the center.

Perhaps the painters are not to be blamed; there was confusion about the flag at the beginning, and it continued for years. Immediately after the war, for example, an American almanac published two illustrations of the flag. Each flag had thirteen stars, but one had fourteen stripes and the other fifteen.

A new problem arose when Vermont was admitted to the Union as a state in 1791, and Kentucky the following year. Both of the new states naturally demanded that they be represented in the country's flag, and the flagmakers were more confused than ever. Should the flag now have fifteen stars and fifteen stripes? Or thirteen stripes and fifteen stars? Or thirteen stars and fifteen stripes?

The problem had to be solved, and it was up to the government to do it.

Fifteen Stars and Stripes

In 1794 the Congress of the United States met at Philadelphia, which was once again the national capital. An unusual debate took place in the House of Representatives—a debate about the demand of Vermont and Kentucky to be recognized in the flag. Before the House was a bill that had already been passed by the Senate. It had been introduced on December 26, 1793, by Stephen R. Bradley, the senior senator from Vermont. The bill read, in part:

"Be it enacted, that from and after the first day of May, Anno Domini one thousand seven hundred and ninety-five, the flag of the United States be fifteen stripes, alternate red and white. That the Union be fifteen stars, white in a blue field . . . "

The Senate had passed the measure unanimously and without debate. But when it reached the House of Representatives, it aroused a storm of angry argument. Congressman George Thacher of Massachusetts called it "a piece of frivolity . . . unworthy of mention in this august body." Congressman Isaac Smith also opposed the bill, even though he was himself from Vermont. He said changing the flag would cost too much. No benefit would come to his state if the government spent a "fortune" on new flags; the money could be put to "a better usage." Vermont did not need such "trivialities" as a star and a stripe. "We are proud to be part of this great Union," he declared, "and do not require petty reminders of our obligations to it."

The most outspoken critic of the bill was Congressman Benjamin Goodhue of Massachusetts. He predicted that in the years to come the United States would grow until it had twenty states, and perhaps more. "Shall we throw out all the old flags every time we welcome a new member into our glorious family?" he asked. "If we continue adding a star and a stripe each time, the flag may have more stripes than a zebra and more stars than in the Heavens! Gentlemen, I exaggerate, but I seriously warn you that if this strange practice is carried out, the beloved Stars and Stripes will become the laughing stock of the world!"

Despite the bitter opposition, the House passed the bill, 50–42, on January 8, 1794. Less than a week later, President Washington signed it and it became law. The nation's first five Presidents—George Washington, John Adams, Thomas Jefferson, James Madison, and James Monroe—served under the flag which bore fifteen stars and fifteen stripes. Although five states were admitted to the Union during their years in office, none won immediate representation in the flag by either a star or a stripe.

The flag of fifteen stars and fifteen stripes was involved in many historical events. While John Adams was President, it was carried in an undeclared naval war against France, which had been the Americans' ally in their fight for independence. The differences between the two countries were soon settled, and the United States emerged as a strong sea power. The flag flew from three great naval frigates—the *United States,* the *Constellation,* and the *Constitution.*

On November 17, 1800, the flag was raised for the first time over the Capitol at Washington, D.C., when Congress met in the building, also for the first time. Three years later, on December 20, 1803, the Stars and Stripes replaced the tricolor of France in New Orleans, which was included in the vast Louisiana Territory

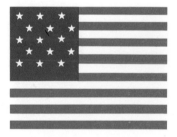

FIFTEEN STARS,
FIFTEEN STRIPES

which the United States had purchased from France. The following spring, President Jefferson sent Meriwether Lewis and William Clark on an expedition to explore the nation's new lands. Lewis and Clark carried the flag to the Pacific Coast, and for the first time the Stars and Stripes waved on both shores of the continent.

Meanwhile, ships were carrying the flag to distant places never before visited by American vessels. In 1800 Captain William Bainbridge took the frigate *George Washington* through the Bosporus to the ancient city of Constantinople, whose name was later changed to Istanbul. The Turkish port officials at Constantinople were at first hostile; they had no knowledge of either the flag or the nation it symbolized. Bainbridge finally managed to make them understand that he came "with friendship in his heart" from that "New World discovered so long ago by the famous navigator, the Admiral of the Seas—Christopher Columbus." The Turks' attitude then changed, and the entire ship's company was entertained by the Sultan, who showered gifts upon the delighted Americans.

Even as Bainbridge was receiving a royal welcome at Constantinople, ships of the United States Navy were battling the Barbary Pirates who operated out of Tripoli in North Africa. For years the pirates had been attacking foreign shipping in the Mediterranean, and American vessels were among those sunk, captured, or plundered. The United States launched a naval campaign against the Tripolitanians, and it did not end until 1805, when United States Marines, supported by warships, captured the Tripolitanian stronghold of Derna. Men of the American landing force lowered the enemy's colors and ran up the Stars and Stripes. This marked the first time the American flag had been raised over an enemy bastion.

But the flag would soon be carried in other battles, in war against the old enemy, Britain.

The Constitution, *carrying the Stars and Stripes, defeats the British ship* Java *during the War of 1812.*

Francis Scott Key wrote The Star-Spangled Banner *during the British bombardment of Fort McHenry.*

In the early 1800's, Britain was at war with Napoleon. In their attempt to defeat France, the British sometimes harassed American merchant ships on the high seas. President James Madison, influenced by a strong war party in the United States, called for a declaration of war, and on June 19, 1812, the United States went to war against Britain. Some Americans called the war "Mr. Madison's War," others called it the "Second War of American Independence," but in time it became known as the War of 1812.

Although the Americans were beaten in one land battle after another, they scored a number of important victories at sea. Daring naval commanders such as William Bainbridge, Charles Stewart, Isaac Hull, Oliver Hazard Perry, and Stephen Decatur led the Stars and Stripes to triumph over the Royal Navy.

The most notable American victory took place on Lake Erie, where Commodore Perry's squadron routed a powerful British force. After the battle, Perry sent this message: "We have met the enemy and they are ours!" His words became famous, as did the last words spoken by Captain James Lawrence. In June of 1813, Lawrence's frigate, the *Chesapeake*, was badly damaged in a battle against the British man-of-war *Shannon*. Mortally wounded, Lawrence cried out, "Don't give up the ship!" His words failed to save the *Chesapeake*, but they have inspired American naval men ever since.

The Star-Spangled Banner

PERRY'S FLAG

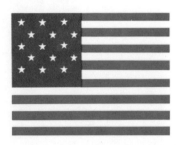

"THE STAR-SPANGLED
BANNER"

A ship was named for Lawrence, and from its mast flew a special flag that bore his words in white against a blue field. The *Lawrence* became Commodore Perry's flagship, and on September 10, 1813, Perry sailed out on Lake Erie to engage the enemy. During the battle, the *Lawrence* was lost, but Perry escaped in a rowboat to another ship, the *Niagara,* and fought on to victory.

It was during the War of 1812 that the frigate *Constitution* won her nickname of "Old Ironsides," when solid shot from the British ship *Guerrière* bounced off her deck. The *Constitution* is preserved today at the Boston Naval Yard, where it still flies a flag of fifteen stars and fifteen stripes.

But the most famous flag of the War of 1812 was flown over Fort McHenry in Baltimore, where the British staged a land-and-sea assault on September 12–14, 1814. Measuring thirty feet by forty-two feet, it was sewn by two Baltimore seamstresses, Mrs. Mary Pickersgill and her daughter. The flag cost $405.90. Colonel George Armistead, commander of the fort, paid for it out of his own money, because there were no government funds available for a flag.

Early on September 13, 1814, the British ships began a bombardment of the fort which went on throughout that day and the following night. A witness of the bombardment was a young Baltimore lawyer named Francis Scott Key, who watched it from the deck of the British warship *Minden.* He and a companion had boarded the vessel to plead with the British commander for the release of Dr. William Beanes, who had been taken prisoner. The commander agreed to set Beanes free, but ordered the Americans to remain on the ship until after the assault on Fort McHenry.

The British used rockets as well as cannon in their attack, and when night came flame seemed to burst from the big guns and the rockets made fiery arcs against the sky. The ship trembled from the roar of the guns, and a cloud of smoke hid the fort. All night Key nervously paced the deck of the *Minden.* How could the Americans hold out against such a fierce attack? He peered through the darkness, hoping to see in the red glare of the rockets that the Stars and Stripes was still there. At daybreak, a fresh wind sprang up. The smoke lifted, revealing the Stars and Stripes waving over the fort.

Using the back of an envelope, Key wrote a tribute to the flag, a poem he called *The Star-Spangled Banner.* Set to the music of an old English drinking song, it quickly became popular, and soon it was being sung wherever Americans gathered. In 1931 an act of Congress made it the national anthem.

The original Star-Spangled Banner—the flag that flew over Fort McHenry—was presented by Colonel Armistead's grandson to the Smithsonian Institution in 1912. Eleven holes had been torn in it by shot fired by the British during the attack. It differed widely in design from later flags; it had fifteen stripes and fifteen five-pointed stars arranged in staggered rows of three each.

Still surviving are two other flags that saw service in the War of 1812. One is the Stonington Flag, which is in the Old Stone Bank at Stonington, Connecticut. It flew from the spire of the courthouse in August of 1814, when ships of the Royal Navy bombarded the town. According to tradition, the townspeople nailed the flag to the flagpole so that no one could lower it in surrender. Surprisingly, it has sixteen stripes and sixteen stars. Just as surprising is the flag that was raised over Fort Hill, Maine, and is now preserved at the Smithsonian Institution. Its fifteen stars are scattered about the canton without alignment and in no special order.

In one form or another, the flag of fifteen stars and fifteen stripes remained official for twenty-three years and two months. This version of the Stars and Stripes holds a unique place in history; it is the only flag that has ever inspired a national anthem.

STONINGTON FLAG

FT. HILL FLAG

A New
Flag Law

The names of Peter Wendover and Captain Samuel Reid are known to few people who are not scholars of American history. And yet these two all but forgotten men were responsible for the development of the modern American flag. It was they who produced the Flag Law which has been in effect since July 4, 1818.

By the end of the War of 1812, many Americans realized that the Flag Law of 1795 was no longer satisfactory. A number of new states had been admitted to the Union since that date, and they were demanding that they be represented in the flag. Peter Wendover, a first-term Congressman from New York, called for a new law to create a national flag that truly represented "all states both present and future." Most Congressmen had little interest in the matter, but Wendover persuaded them that action was needed. They appointed him chairman of a special committee to study "the flag problem," and he devoted all his energies to the task.

It was clearly impractical to add both a star and a stripe every time a new state joined the Union. In a report to Congress, Wendover wrote, "Should that practise be followed our flag would resemble nothing else than peppermint shirting . . . Of necessity, the stripes would have to be ever narrower until they were little more than thin red lines."

Seeking a solution, Wendover consulted a friend, Captain Samuel Reid, a naval hero of the War of 1812. Captain Reid offered a number of suggestions. Many of them were of little value, but one struck Wendover as making good sense. The number of stripes, Reid said, should remain at thirteen to represent the original states. For each existing state, one star should appear in the canton. A new star would be added whenever a new state gained admission to the Union.

Wendover presented this idea to Congress in the form of a bill, but the House adjourned without taking action on it. Wendover was not discouraged. He brought up the bill again at the next session of Congress, in December of 1817. To win support for it, he pointed out the wide differences in existing flags. Over a wing of the Capitol flew a flag of thirteen stars and thirteen stripes. Other government buildings in Washington displayed Stars and Stripes in a variety of designs. One bore nine stars and nine stripes; another, eighteen stars and eighteen stripes.

"This situation borders on anarchy," Wendover said. "As we are one distinctive nation, so must we have one distinctive flag."

His remarks unloosed a flood of suggestions from Congressmen, who called for seven, nine, thirteen, and eleven stars and stripes. Wendover saw that such suggestions were worthless. He held to his plan, and on March 25, 1818, he placed his bill before Congress.

In its final draft, the bill, entitled *An Act To Establish The Flag Of The United States*, read, in part:

> Section 1. Be it enacted that from and after the fourth of July next, the flag of the United States be thirteen horizontal stripes, alternate red and white; that the union have twenty stars, white, in a blue field . . . Section 2. And be it further enacted, that on the admission of every new state into the Union, one star be added to the union of the flag; and that such addition . . . shall take effect on the fourth of July next succeeding such admission . . .

Wendover's bill was passed in the House, with only a few votes cast against it. It did even better in the Senate, where it was passed unanimously. The measure became law when it was signed on April 4, 1818, by President James Monroe.

Under the new Flag Law, the stripes were to remain thirteen in number and be placed horizontally. The number of stars was limited only by the number of states in the Union. Their arrangement within the can-

EIGHTEEN STARS,
EIGHTEEN STRIPES

Americans moving west meant new states and new stars for the flag.

TWENTY STARS,
THIRTEEN STRIPES

ton was still left undecided. Wendover believed this "should be left to the discretion of persons more immediately concerned, either to set them out in form of one great luminary, or in the words of the original resolution of 1777, representing a new constellation." In other words, the stars could be arranged in the form of a single large star, or in a form "imitating the arrangement of a heavenly body."

Nine days after President Monroe signed the bill, a flag of twenty stars and thirteen stripes was raised over the Capitol. Sewn by Mrs. Samuel Reid, it had the stars arranged as "one great luminary." The first new state to benefit by the law was Illinois; the star recognizing this state was added to the flag on July 4, 1819.

By the time Captain Reid died, at the age of seventy-eight, in 1861, the flag bore thirty-four stars for thirty-four states. Two years before his death, Congress acknowledged his contribution to the development of the Stars and Stripes by giving him a vote of thanks.

From time to time, over the years, there has been talk of amending the law so that it requires a uniform arrangement of the stars. But Congress has never done anything about it. When a state enters the Union, the President of the United States, by Executive Order, determines the arrangement of the stars. Nevertheless, the Flag Law of 1818 brought a degree of uniformity in design, and the Stars and Stripes truly became a national flag.

THIRTY-FOUR STARS

Old Glory

In 1824, when the flag bore twenty-four stars, it received a nickname that is still often used. The name was given to it by Captain William Driver of Salem, Massachusetts. Captain Driver was the master of the schooner *Charles Doggett,* and one day his friends presented him with a beautifully made Stars and Stripes for his vessel. He was so delighted with the gift that he himself immediately hauled up the flag on the mainmast. As the flag rippled in the breeze, Captain Driver cried, "I name thee 'Old Glory'!"

As so often happens with famous flags, a legend later sprang up about the original Old Glory. The story goes that when Captain Driver's native state, Tennessee, seceded from the Union in 1861, the captain, who had long retired from the sea, hid the flag in his Nashville home. In February of the following year, Union troops took Nashville. As the first of the Federals entered the city, they were greeted by Old Glory, waving from the flagpole outside the old captain's house. At any rate, the original Old Glory was presented to the Smithsonian Institution by the Driver family in 1922.

It was not until 1834 that the United States Army officially recognized the Stars and Stripes—fifty years after it had been adopted as the national flag. Army General Regulations for 1834 stated:

TWENTY-FOUR STARS

> The garrison flag is the national flag . . . to be composed of thirteen horizontal stripes of equal breadth, alternately red and white beginning with the red. In the upper quarter, near the staff, will be the Union, composed of a number of white stars, equal to the number of the states, distributed over a blue field, one-third the length of the flag, and to run down to the lower edge of the fourth stripe from the top . . .

In military fashion, the Army tried to standardize the design of the flag. But Army General Regulations failed to mention the arrangement of the stars in the canton, and the Stars and Stripes continued to appear in various forms. Few were as extreme as the flag carried by General John Charles Frémont on his expeditions to the West during the 1840's. Frémont designed a flag with twenty-six stars set in two wavy lines of thirteen each. Between the two lines of stars was an eagle clutching a bundle of arrows and an Indian peace pipe in its talons. Frémont was breaking no law in displaying such a flag, but it aroused considerable unfavorable comment.

Possibly one of the worst blunders involving the flag came during the fall of 1842. It was made by Commodore Thomas ap Catesby Jones, commander of the United States Navy's Pacific Squadron. He mistakenly believed that the United States and Mexico, which were having a dispute over the borders of the two countries, had actually gone to war. He sailed his ships into Monterey Bay, put ashore a strong landing force, seized the town, raised the Stars and Stripes, and proclaimed California a territory of the United States. A few days later, he learned of his mistake. He quietly lowered the Stars and Stripes, ran up the Mexican flag again, and sailed to Los Angeles, where he apologized to the Mexican governor. The governor accepted his apology and entertained him at a ball.

Some three years later, in 1845, war did break out between the United States and Mexico. The war ended with the signing of the Treaty of Guadalupe Hidalgo on February 2, 1848. The United States Senate passed a resolution stating that "the Vice President . . . be requested to have the United States flag first raised by the American army upon the palace in the capital of Mexico deposited for safekeeping in the Department of State of the United States."

The flag mentioned in the resolution was the one carried by the American troops who had stormed the Mexican stronghold of Chapultepec in the assault on Mexico City. This flag had twenty-eight stars arranged in four

In 1853, the Stars and Stripes landed in Japan with Commodore Perry.

56

even rows of seven each. There were now twenty-nine states in the Union, but the war had slowed down the manufacture of flags, and many Army units carried flags with twenty-eight or even twenty-seven stars. As a result of the war, the United States acquired vast new territories, including New Mexico and California. The Gold Rush of 1849 brought more than 80,000 people to California, and Californians were soon demanding admission into the Union as a state. On September 9, 1850, California did indeed become a state, and the following July the thirty-first star was placed on the flag. The thirtieth star, for Wisconsin, had been placed in the canton on July 4, 1848.

The flag of thirty-one stars was carried to Japan by Commodore Matthew C. Perry, whose ship dropped anchor in Tokyo Bay on July 8, 1853. Perry's flag, the first Stars and Stripes to be displayed in Japan, is preserved today in the Museum of the United States Naval Academy. Three Presidents—Millard Fillmore, Franklin Pierce, and James Buchanan—served under the thirty-one-star flag, and during the seven years of its existence the danger of civil war between the North and the South daily grew more threatening. In spite of this, the country continued to expand. Minnesota brought the thirty-second star to the flag on July 4, 1858, and a year later Oregon brought the thirty-third. The United States was now a vast country whose lands stretched from ocean to ocean.

And yet, within two years, eleven of the thirty-three states had left the Union. They set up a government of their own, the Confederate States of America, with a flag of its own. The break between the North and the South came in 1860, with the election of Abraham Lincoln to the Presidency of the United States. Even so, on January 29, 1861, a thirty-fourth state, Kansas, was admitted. By July fourth, when its star was placed on the flag, the nation was torn by a terrible and bloody war.

THIRTY-ONE STARS

THIRTY-THREE STARS

The Civil War began on April 12, 1861. On that day the guns of the South Carolina artillery bombarded Fort Sumter, a Federal installation in Charleston Harbor.

After a bombardment of thirty-four hours—one hour for each star then in the flag—the fort could no longer hold out. Major Robert Anderson, the fort's commander, hauled down the Stars and Stripes in surrender. The next day he and his men left their post. Before leaving, he again raised the flag and honored it with a fifty-gun salute. Curiously, the only casualty of the battle took place during the ceremony; one of the cannon firing the salute burst, and a Union soldier was killed.

Major Anderson then hauled down the flag, carefully folded it, and placed it in his mapcase. It went with him when he marched out of the fort with his troops; the Southerners had given them permission to take their weapons and personal belongings. Ships of the United States Navy picked up the Union soldiers and carried them away from Charleston.

In response to the attack on Fort Sumter, President Abraham Lincoln called for 75,000 volunteers to put down the Southern "insurrection." The Southerners, too, mobilized their forces, and Americans faced each other on the battle lines. Both sides expected that the fighting would soon be over. They were mistaken. And, as the war dragged on and casualties mounted, feeling between the North and the South grew even more bitter. In the North, a number of people wanted the eleven stars of the seceded states removed from the flag. Some Northern flagmakers produced an unofficial flag of twenty-three stars. A few went so far as to produce flags of nineteen stars, excluding not only the seceding states, but also the slave-holding border states of Delaware, Kentucky, Maryland, and Missouri.

Many proposals, most of them far-fetched, were made

The Flag and the Civil War

THIRTY-FOUR STARS

Abraham Lincoln said that all states still belonged to the Union and that the flag would remain as it was with thirty-four stars in it.

THIRTY-FIVE STARS

FIRST CONFEDERATE
FLAG

CONFEDERATE BATTLE
FLAG

LAST CONFEDERATE
FLAG

to change the flag. Samuel F. B. Morse, the inventor of the telegraph, suggested that the Stars and Stripes be divided into two flags—one with twenty-three stars and six-and-a-half stripes, the other with eleven stars and six-and-a-half stripes.

President Lincoln firmly turned down all the proposals. He said that the war was not a war between nations, but a war of a legal government against a rebellion by eleven of its states. He declared that the seceded states still belonged to the Union, whether they liked it or not, and that the flag would remain as it was.

There was one change, however, during the war. On June 20, 1863, several of the northwest counties of Virginia entered the Union as a full-fledged state, called West Virginia. A thirty-fifth star, representing West Virginia, was added to the flag's canton. The demands of the war limited the manufacture of the thirty-five star flag, and most Federal troops fought under the old flag of thirty-four stars.

The war ended in April of 1865, after the Confederate commander, General Robert E. Lee, surrendered to General Ulysses S. Grant at Appomattox Court House in Virginia. The Southern veterans sadly furled the Confederate flag, and a New York newspaper announced in a headline: "The Old Flag Waves from Maine to the Rio Grande." Everywhere in the North the Stars and Stripes was carried in victory celebrations.

On April 14, 1865, precisely four years after they had marched out of Fort Sumter, Federal troops returned to the fort. Major Robert Anderson—now a Major General —raised over the fort the flag he had hauled down in 1861. As the Stars and Stripes caught the breeze, a great crowd of spectators cheered and applauded, and a hundred guns boomed in a thunderous salute.

That same night, President Lincoln was shot. He died the next morning. The flags of the nation were lowered to half-mast.

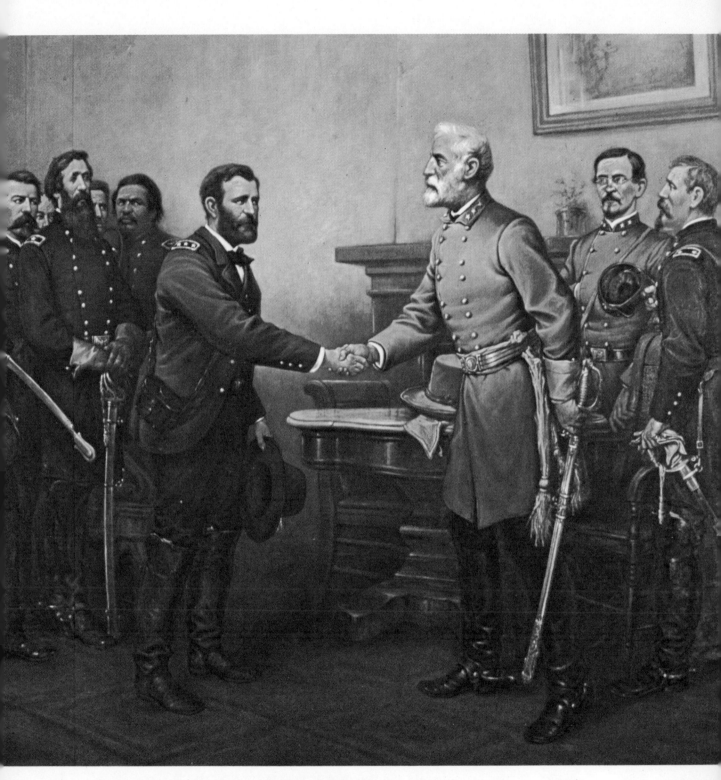

Lee's surrender to Grant in 1865 marked the end of the Civil War. A northern newspaper announced, "The Old Flag Waves from Maine to the Rio Grande."

The Flag in War and Peace

After the Civil War, the flag once again waved over a unified nation, but the wounds of war healed slowly. The shattered South had to be rebuilt, and Yankee and Rebel had to learn to live together as Americans. The period of adjustment lasted until about 1877—and then the country moved forward with giant strides, growing at an astonishing rate. From an agricultural nation, the United States was transformed into an industrial nation. A land of farms became a land of factories, mines, mills, and railroads. More states came into the Union, and more stars were added to the flag.

For thirty-three years, the longest such span in the nation's history, the United States took part in no major war. The years of peace came to an end in 1898, when the American battleship *Maine* was blown up in Havana harbor, taking the lives of 260 men. Although the cause of the disaster was not known, the blame was placed on Spain, which was putting down a revolt against its rule in Cuba. Already sympathetic to the Cubans, Americans were soon shouting the slogan, "Remember the Maine!" Newspapers helped whip up the war spirit, and on April 21, 1898, the United States declared war on Spain.

The Americans won an easy victory over the Spanish. At the peace table, Spain ceded Puerto Rico, the Philippine Islands, and Guam to the United States. A nation which had grown from thirteen colonies now had colonies of its own. The Stars and Stripes, itself born in a revolution, was carried by the American soldiers who were sent to crush an uprising in the Philippines in 1899. The power of the United States extended beyond its continental frontiers, and in 1907 a squadron of sixteen United States Navy battleships set out on a globe-encircling voyage "to show the flag." The Stars and Stripes then bore forty-five stars, but within a year a forty-sixth star, representing Oklahoma, was added to the canton. It was the forty-six star flag that was raised at the top of the world by Admiral Robert E. Peary, who reached the North Pole on April 6, 1909.

Three years later, New Mexico and Arizona became states, and there were forty-eight stars in the canton. The flag would remain unchanged for forty-seven years, through the administrations of Presidents William Howard Taft, Woodrow Wilson, Warren G. Harding, Calvin Coolidge, Herbert Hoover, Franklin D. Roosevelt, and Harry S. Truman, and through part of the administration of President Dwight D. Eisenhower.

It was during the administration of William Howard Taft, who served as President from 1909 to 1913, that the government officially established the proportions of the flag. This action was taken after a survey showed that the flag was being made in sixty-six different sizes, and with a variety of arrangements of the stars in the canton. In two executive orders, dated June 24 and October 29, 1912, President Taft set specific standards for "the sizes of flags manufactured or purchased for Government Departments." Accompanying the October executive order was a plan furnished by the Navy Department showing the exact design of the flag, including the arrangement of the stars in the canton. Twenty-two years later, the exact shades of color to be used in the flag were also specified. At last, after so many years, standards had been set for the appearance of the flag.

The forty-eight star flag was carried into combat in 1917, against Germany in World War I, and flew in several sectors of the Western Front. It also flew in Siberia, when American troops were sent to Archangel as part of an anti-Communist Expeditionary Force. After World War I, in the 1920's, the flag waved over a land of great prosperity. That prosperity ended with the

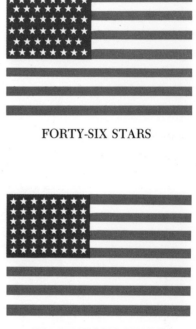

FORTY-SIX STARS

FORTY-EIGHT STARS

The United States Marines raised the Stars and Stripes on Iwo Jima during World War II. The flag now flies night and day at the Marine Corps Memorial, in Arlington, Virginia, commemorating this battle.

stock market crash of October, 1929. Then came the Great Depression of the 1930's, and the flag was carried in demonstrations by the unemployed.

By 1941 the United States was again at war, and the Stars and Stripes was again under fire. Sometimes it was hauled down in defeat, as at Bataan and Corregidor, but in the end it was raised in victory, in both Europe and the Pacific, and it billowed triumphantly over the American troops who took part in the occupation of the enemy countries. The Stars and Stripes went to war again in 1950, in Korea, this time flying beside the blue and white banner of the United Nations.

On July 4, 1959, a forty-ninth star was added to the canton, for Alaska, and a year later a fiftieth, for Hawaii. The fifty stars are arranged in the canton in alternate rows of six and five, staggered, with five rows of six stars and four rows of five. The fifty-star flag was the flag draped over the coffin of President John F. Kennedy, after he was assassinated in 1963. In the late 1960's it, too, was carried into battle, in far-off Viet Nam. When American space vehicles went blasting off on fantastic journeys, their rockets' red glare gave proof that the flag was still there—painted on the sides of the vehicles, or on the sleeves of the space suits worn by the astronauts. The Stars and Stripes, which had been displayed at so many places on the earth, was displayed in space, and Americans were looking foward to the day when it would be planted on the moon.

The flag had grown from thirteen stars to fifty, the nation had grown from thirteen struggling states to a great world power. As a world power, it had immense accomplishments to be proud of—and immense problems to be faced. But the Stars and Stripes remained the symbol of the ideal of freedom and democracy, a constant reminder that, as Abraham Lincoln said, "government of the people, by the people, and for the people, shall not perish from the earth."

FIFTY STARS

65

The Use of the Flag

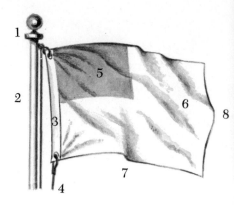

The flag is flown 24 hours a day at the following places:

by Presidential Proclamation

> Fort McHenry, Maryland
> Flaghouse Square, Baltimore, Maryland
> U.S. Capitol, Washington D.C.
> Marine Corps Memorial, Arlington, Virginia

by tradition

> Francis Scott Key's Grave, Frederick, Maryland
> War Memorial, Worcester, Massachusetts
> The Plaza, Taos, New Mexico
> Civilian Cemetery, Deadwood, South Dakota

During good weather the flag may be properly displayed from sunrise to sunset. The following dates are considered flag holidays:

> New Year's Day, January 1
> Inauguration Day, January 20
> Lincoln's Birthday, February 12
> Washington's Birthday, February 22
> Easter Sunday (date changes each year)
> Mother's Day, second Sunday in May
> Armed Forces Day, third Saturday in May
> Memorial Day (half-staff until noon), May 30
> Flag Day, June 14
> Independence Day, July 4
> Labor Day, first Monday in September
> Constitution and Citizenship Day, September 17
> Columbus Day, October 12
> Veterans Day, November 11
> Thanksgiving Day, fourth Thursday in November
> Christmas Day, December 25

Such other days as may be proclaimed by the President of the United States.

> Birthdays (dates of admission) of States
> State holidays

PARTS OF A FLAG

1 Truck
2 Mast, Flagpole, or Flagstaff
3 Hoist
4 Halyard
5 Canton or Union
6 Field or Ground
7 Fly
8 Fly End

66

The flag should be raised and lowered only by hand. It should be unfurled, then raised quickly and lowered slowly.

When the flag is to be flown at half-mast, it should be raised to the top of the pole first and then lowered to half-mast. Before the flag is taken down for the day, it should be momentarily raised to the top of the pole.

When the flag is carried, it should always be free and aloft—never flat.

When the flag is carried in any kind of procession, it should be on the right of the marchers. If several other flags are being carried, the United States flag may be carried in front of the center of them.

When the flag is displayed over the center of a street, it should be hung vertically with the union to the north on east-west streets. On north-south streets the union should be to the east.

When the flag passes in a parade, or when it is being raised or lowered, civilians salute it by putting their right hands over their hearts and standing at attention.

When a number of city, state, or society flags are used on staffs with the flag of the United States, the latter flag must be in the center and higher than the other flags.

If only one other flag is used with the flag of the United States and the staffs are crossed, the flag of the United States is placed on the flag's right with its staff in front of the other flag's.

A speaker's table should never be covered with the flag. On a staff the flag may appear at the speaker's right. If the flag is placed flat on the wall behind the speaker, the union is to the flag's right.

Nothing should ever be placed on or over the flag. It should never be used as a receptacle. A flag no longer suitable for display should be burned in a dignified way. The flag should never touch the ground.

No flag should be placed above that of the United States except the U.N. flag at the United Nations headquarters. When flags of several nations are used, they should be of the same size and flown from separate poles of the same height. In time of peace the flag of one nation is not flown above that of another nation.

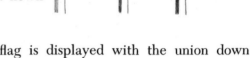

The flag is displayed with the union down only as a signal of utmost distress.

When the flag is not displayed on a pole, it should be flat with the union always to the right of the flag.

The flag should never be used as part of a costume, nor should it be used as a decoration on any object.

Display the flag on a pole from a window with the union at the peak of the pole (except at half-mast).

The flag should never be used for decoration. Blue, white, and red (not red, white and blue) bunting is available for this purpose.

If displayed on a staff in church, on a platform or chancel, it should be to the clergyman's right with any other flags placed to his left. If the flag is displayed on the floor of the church, it should face the congregation's right with any other flags to their left.

No marks, letters or drawings should ever be placed on the flag.

When the flag covers a casket, the union is placed at the head end over the left shoulder. The flag is never permitted to touch the ground; it is not lowered into the grave.